COLOR
your campus

INDIANA
UNIVERSITY

ILLUSTRATED BY

Melissa Mueller

QUARRY BOOKS

an imprint of · Indiana University Press · Bloomington & Indianapolis

*For my mom and dad, who've been with me through every
sketch, charcoal drawing, painting, ink drawing, and art project.
Thank you for encouraging and funding me every step of the way.*

—Melissa Mueller

Quarry Books
an imprint of

Indiana University Press
Office of Scholarly Publishing
Herman B Wells Library 350
1320 East 10th Street
Bloomington, Indiana 47405 USA

iupress.indiana.edu

The paper used in this publication meets the minimum requirements
of the American National Standard for Information Sciences—
Permanence of Paper for Printed Library Materials, ANSI Z39.48-1992.

Manufactured in the United States of America

ISBN 978-0-253-02412-1 (pbk.)

1 2 3 4 5 20 19 18 17 16

PRESS

Sample Gates

Student Building

Franklin Hall

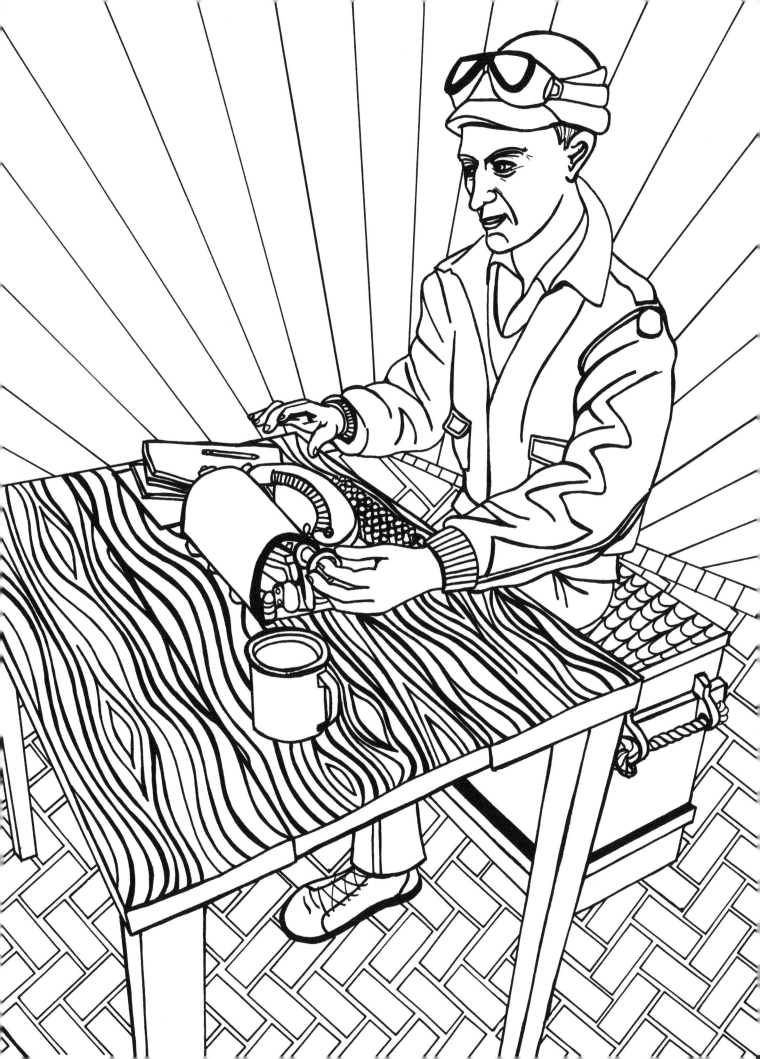

Ernie Pyle statue

Rose Well House

Kirkwood
Observatory

Kirkwood Observatory

Jordan River

PRESS

Dunn Meadow

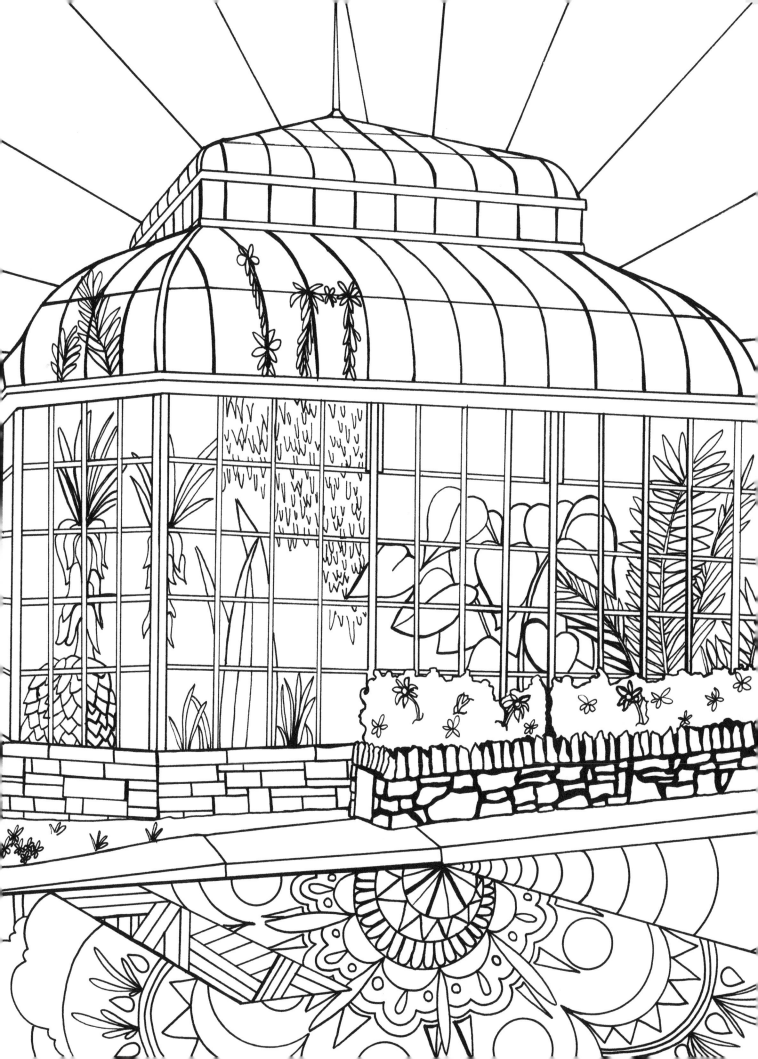

Jordan Hall Greenhouse

Indiana Memorial Union

Indiana Memorial Union Bowling & Billiards

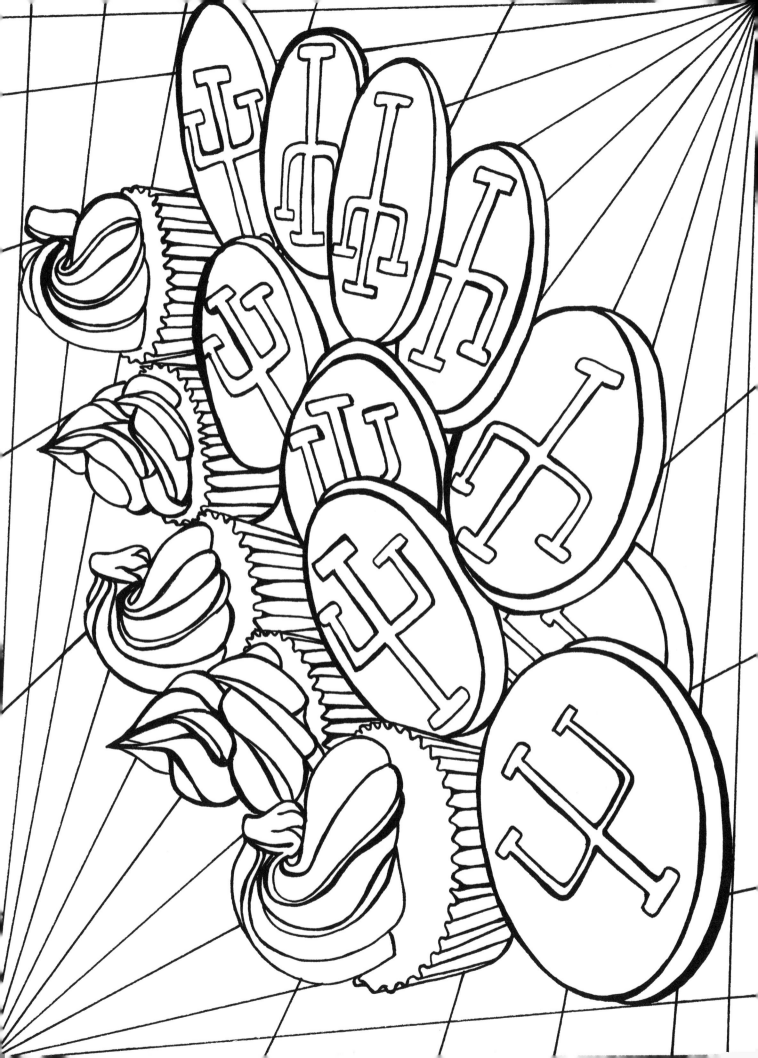

Beck Chapel

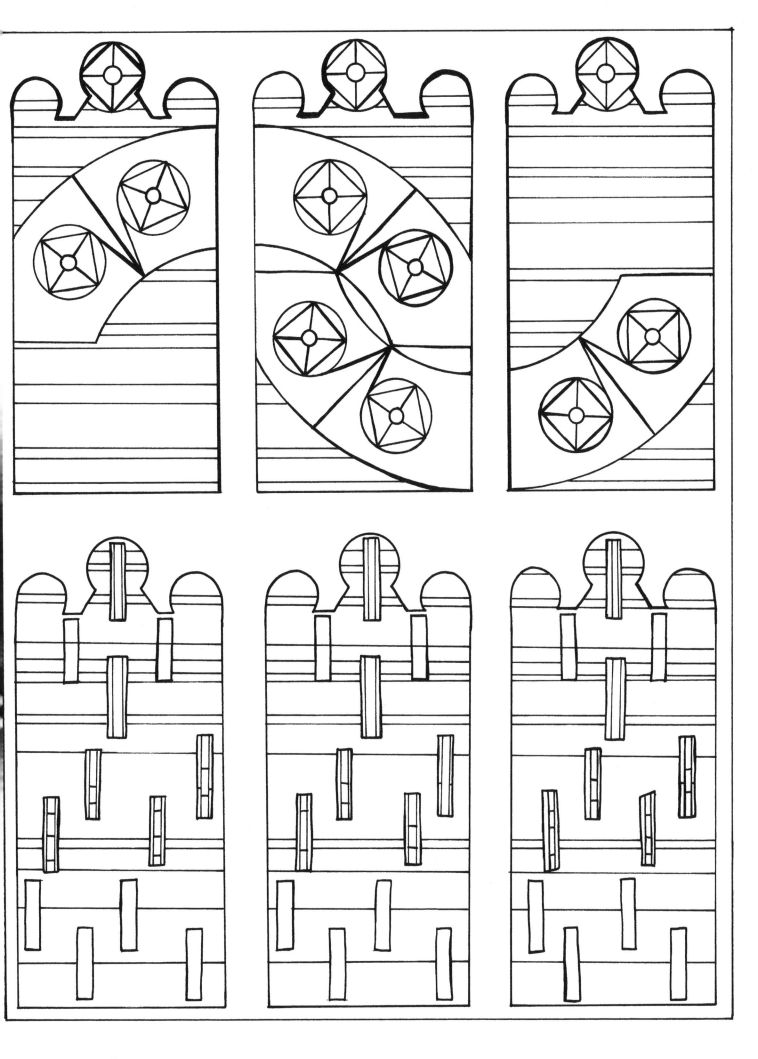

Beck Chapel's stained glass

The Eskenazi Museum of Art exterior

The Eskenazi Museum of Art interior

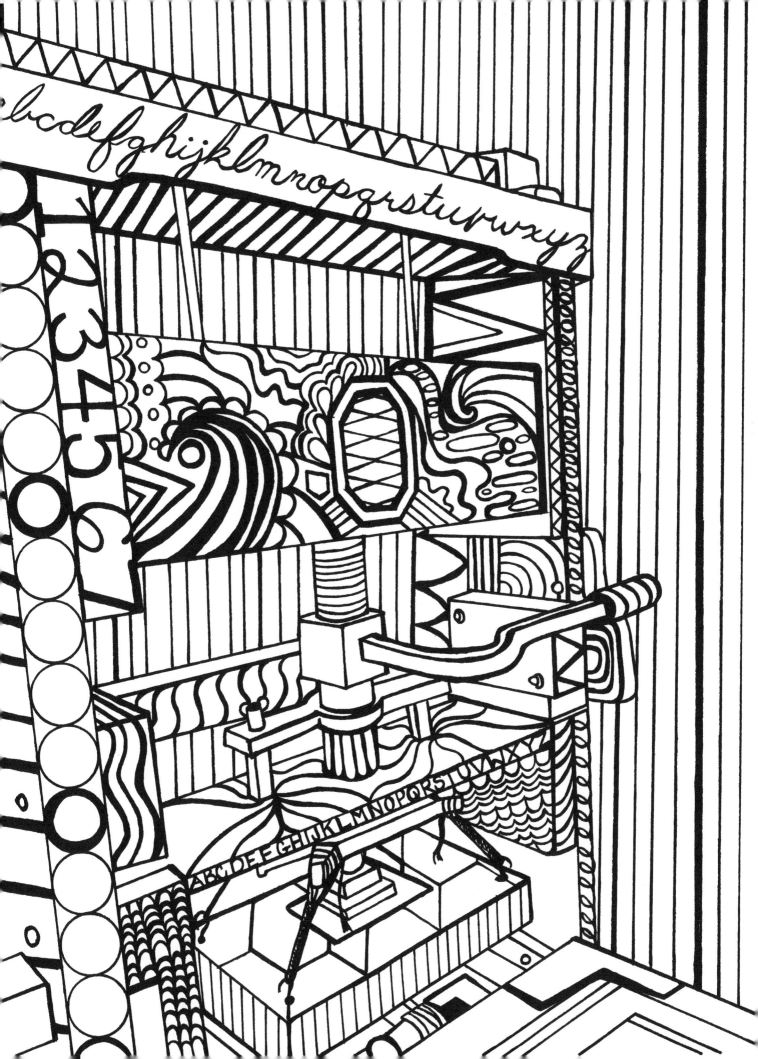

Lilly Library's printing press

Indiana University Auditorium and Showalter Fountain

Indiana University Cinema

Bryan House

Hoagy Carmichael statue

Jacobs School of Music Recital Hall

Jacobs School of Music Ford-Crawford Hall

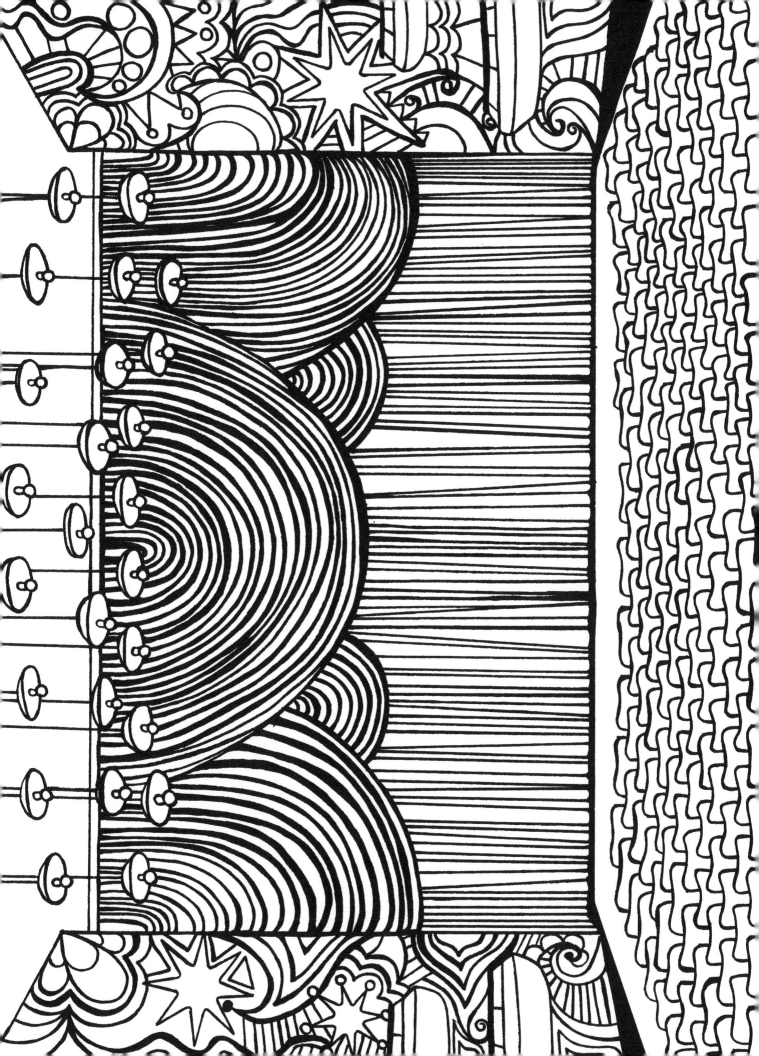

Musical Arts Center

Leo R. Dowling International Center

School of Education

PRESS

Herman B Wells statue

School of Global and International Studies

Arboretum Gazebo

Chemistry Building

Kelley School of Business Hodge Hall Undergraduate Center

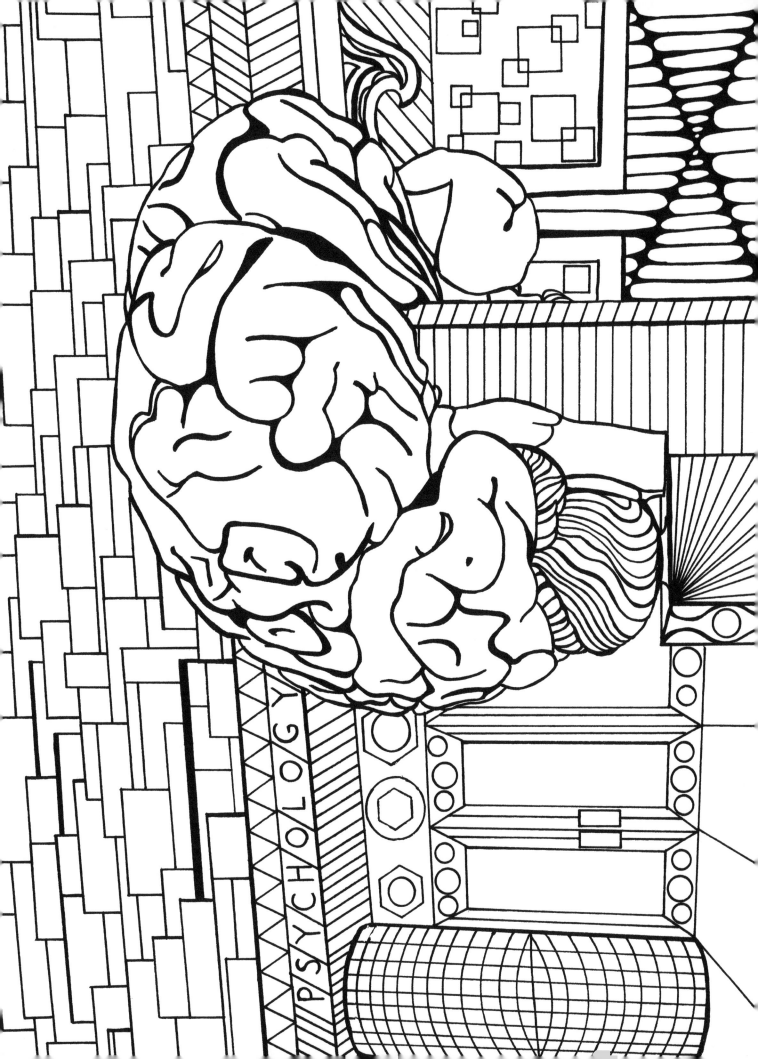

Department of Psychological & Brain Studies Building

Arthur R. Metz Memorial Carillon

Student Recreational Sports Center

Counsilman/Billingsley Aquatic Center

PRESS

Memorial Stadium's The Rock

PRESS

Cook Hall

Assembly Hall court

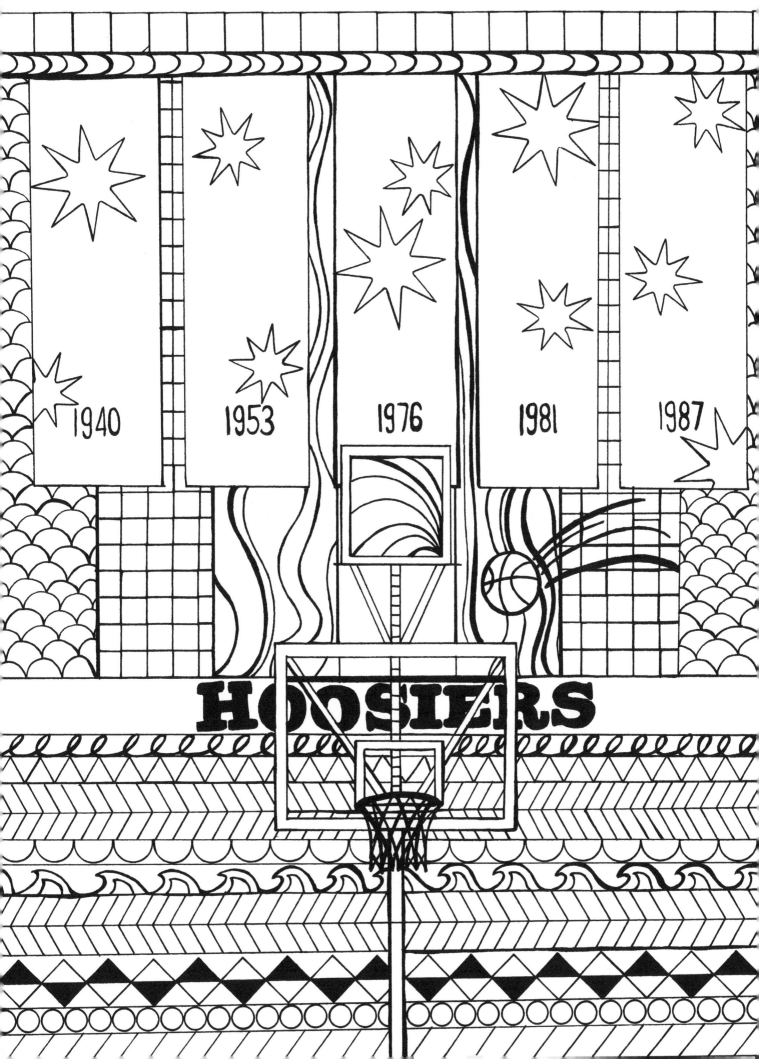

Assembly Hall banners

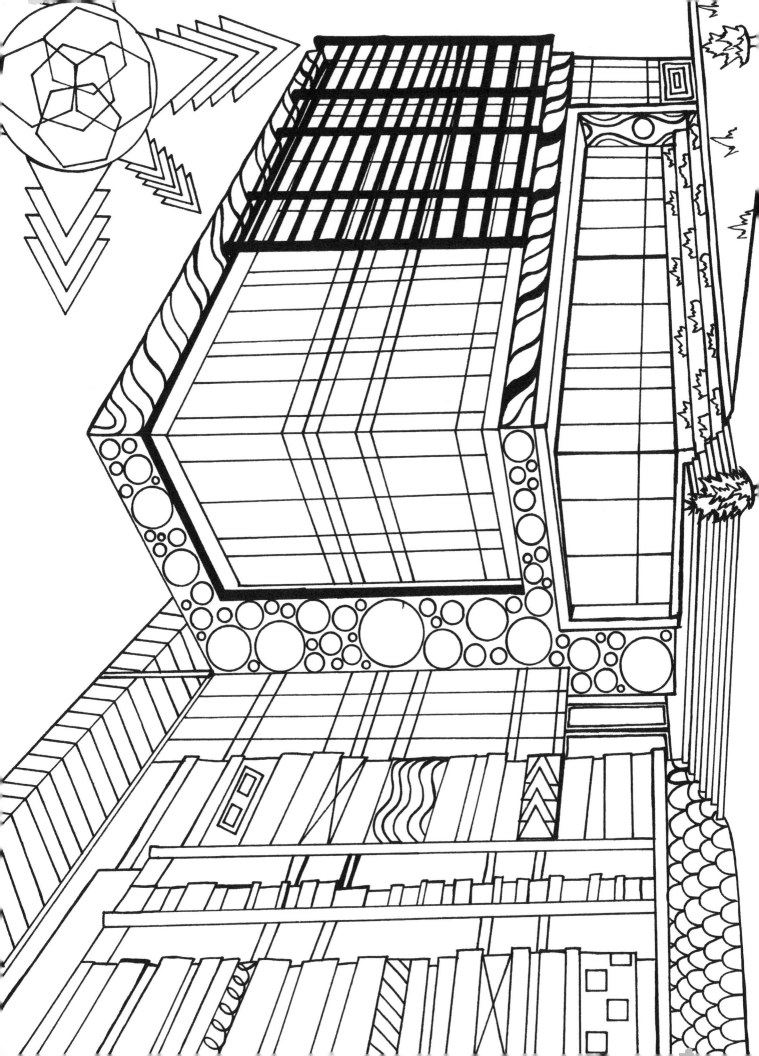

PRESS

Cyberinfrastructure Building